Coloring, My Style

I've always preferred to paint in a realistic sty[le]
find animals and nature so beautiful just the [way they are that I don't feel]
the need to add to or subtract anything fro[m my]
artwork, I want to share this natural beauty I see in my subjects. For
most of my life I painted with traditional oils. I preferred oils over other
mediums because oils gave me rich, deep colors and fine detail that
brought my animal subjects to life. In recent years I've also started
doing artwork on the computer. Here are some examples of art I've
done to get you inspired. Don't worry, though—you can achieve
a stunning array of colors using more common, classic media like
markers and colored pencils. I hope my style and the samples on the
following pages inspire you!

Detail of an owl's eye painted digitally

*Detail of an elk's eye, ear, and antler
painted in traditional oils*

Finding the Rainbow in Earth Tones

When we think of what we call "earth tones," we often imagine various shades of browns and grays. But earth tones really include all the colors of the rainbow. Of course we notice that flowers come in all sorts of bright colors, but it's often different when we think of animals. It's easy to look at the image below and see just a brown bird with black spots. It really doesn't have any color other than the red spot on the back of its head, right?

In reality, even these "plain" browns can have other colors in them, because everything reflects the light that bounces off surrounding objects. The pinks from the flowers, the greens from the foliage, the blues from the sky, and shadows all change the colors of these browns and grays.

I've taken some swatches from different areas of the bird so you can better see the true color variations. The browns actually include red, orange, yellow, green, and blue tones.

So as you're coloring a brown or gray bird, don't just go straight for the brown or gray colored pencils. Use those colors as the base colors, but then layer a little bit of another color over them. Layer them with the colors you're using in the flowers, foliage, and sky to make your artwork more vibrant, interesting, and realistic.

Northern Flicker

Making Color Choices

I like to color realistically because I think nature and animals are beautiful the way they are. But sometimes it's fun to go crazy and color things in completely unnatural ways. Here I've colored this bird and background both realistically and in fun rainbow colors.

You certainly don't have to color any bird realistically. Feel free to use any or all the colors of the rainbow, as I've done below.

Hermit Thrush

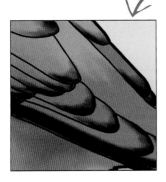

When coloring realistically, don't forget the subtle shade variations such as those seen on the wing feathers here. This isn't just a plain, solid brown bird!

Experiment with adding your own textures and patterns, as shown here on the wing and the background, to make it even more fun and expressive of your own style.

Tips for Coloring Feathers

When coloring feathers, take note of the texture and color variations within the feathers as well as the different types of feathers on different parts of the bird.

Baltimore Oriole

On the body and head of a bird, individual feathers are harder to discern. These feathers sometimes look more like soft, fine fur than feathers. You can see this texture in the edges and highlights. You can add interest to dark- or solid-colored birds by adding these lighter highlights and edge textures.

Highlighting edges helps you see individual feathers on dark birds that might otherwise blend together.

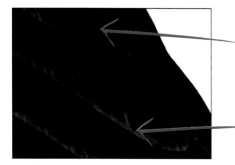

On a bird's wings, it's usually easy to see the individual feathers. These larger wing feathers usually have a distinctive shaft down the center that is lighter or darker than the main part of the feather. The fibers of the feather fan out from this shaft.

The edges of feathers are often lighter in color, either from the bird's natural color variation or due to the wear and tear of wind and weather on the feather's edges.

Creating Highlights and Shading with Blending

To create nice shaded and highlighted effects, use three different shades of a single color and blend them together. Follow along with the flower coloring steps below to learn how to do this. It's best to try it out first with a colored pencil if you're new to this technique.

1 Start by filling in the image using the lightest shades you want to see. Here, I did a light green for the leaves and a pale lavender for the flowers. I also left some areas white so that I can have a bright highlight effect. I left the center of the flowers blank for now.

2 Add the middle tones with a darker shade. This creates the medium color of the area.

3 Add the darkest tones with your darkest shade. It's better to use a dark shade of your "master" color for the darkest shadow areas, not black. This creates the deep, shadowed areas that give depth to a design.

4 Finish by adding smaller elements and details as desired. I added color to the center of the flowers and very fine pencil lines to the petals.

Eastern Bluebird, page 79.

Colored pencils (Prismacolor), watercolor pencils (Master's Touch). Color by Darla Tjelmeland.

Black-capped Chickadee, page 45.
Brush markers (Zig by Kuretake), colored pencils (Derwent Inktense), soft pastels. Color by Lisa Caryl.

California Gull, page 31.

8   *Colored pencils (Prismacolor), watercolor pencils. Color by Darla Tjelmeland.*

Baltimore Oriole, page 53.
Colored pencils (Prismacolor), gel pens (Sakura). Color by Kelly Nagorka.   9

Common Loon, page 29.

Colored pencils (Prismacolor), watercolor pencils (Master's Touch). Color by Darla Tjelmeland.

Purple Finch, page 77.
Colored pencils (Faber-Castell). Color by Katja Lahti. 11

Western Meadowlark, page 51.

12 *Colored pencils (Prismacolor), watercolor pencils (Master's Touch). Color by Darla Tjelmeland.*

Northern Mockingbird, page 69.
Colored pencils (Prismacolor), soft pastels. Color by Lisa Caryl. 13

Northern Flicker, page 41.

Colored pencils (Prismacolor), watercolor pencils. Color by Darla Tjelmeland.

Cactus Wren, page 47.
Colored pencils (Marco Raffine and Crayola), pastels (Mungyo). Color by Keara Irby.   15

Brown Pelican, page 43.

16   *Colored pencils (Prismacolor), watercolor pencils (Master's Touch). Color by Darla Tjelmeland.*

Brown Thrasher

(Toxostoma rufum)

Brown thrashers can imitate over 1,000 strings of music, including many from other bird species, which makes its songs some of the most complex of the songbirds.

American Robin

(Turdus migratorius)

The American robin often signals the end of winter and the beginning of spring because it is one of the first birds to leave its roost and search the ground for insects to eat.

Steller's Jay. © Design Originals, *www.D-Originals.com*

Steller's Jay

(Cyanocitta stelleri)

Steller's jays have a large "family": this bird species, Steller's sea lion, Steller's eider, Steller's sea cow, and Steller's sea eagle were all discovered by naturalist Georg Steller on an expedition to Alaska.

23

Willow Ptarmigan

(Lagopus lagopus)

Willow ptarmigans are very social creatures, for they can often be seen playing with one another through jumping, flapping, and head bobbing. Their flocks can grow to over 2,000 birds!

American Goldfinch

(Spinus tristis)

Unlike most birds, the American goldfinch doesn't eat meat or insects (except by accident). Instead, it sticks to seeds, fruits, and grains in order to get nutrients.

Nene

(Branta sandvicensis)

The nene almost went extinct in the 1950s when its population was reduced to about 30 birds. However, conservation efforts have brought that number up to about 2,500 today.

Common Loon

(Gavia immer)

The common loon's feet are farther back on its body than other birds, making it a great swimmer. This unusual anatomy also means that it needs a longer "runway" of water to take to the air.

California Gull. © Crista Forest, *www.foreststudios.com*. From *Birds at Home, Revised Edition* © Design Originals, *www.D-Originals.com*

California Gull

(Larus californicus)

California gulls are actually the state bird of Utah. In 1848, crickets nearly destroyed all the crops in the main Utah settlement, until the gulls ate all the crickets.

33

Carolina Wren

(Thryothorus ludovicianus)

Male Carolina wrens are primarily the singers for this species. Their loud and aggressive songs are used as a way of defending territory and warding off intruders.

Greater Roadrunner

(Geococcyx californianus)

Greater roadrunners are built for running rather than flying.
By leaning its body and tail nearly parallel to the ground, the
roadrunner reaches speeds of 20 mph (32 km/h).

Rock Ptarmigan. © Design Originals, *www.D-Originals.com*

Rock Ptarmigan

(Lagopus muta)

For the rock ptarmigan, winter camouflage differs between the males and females. A male stays white longer, and it often coats itself in dirt until the time when it finally molts to brown.

Northern Cardinal

(Cardinalis cardinalis)

Northern cardinals are some of the most recognizable and beloved songbirds in North America. It used to be a popular pet, but this practice was banned in both Canada and the United States.

Northern Flicker. © Crista Forest, *www.foreststudios.com*. From *Birds at Home, Revised Edition* © Design Originals, *www.D-Originals.com*

Northern Flicker

(Colaptes auratus)

The northern flicker has a distinctive shaft of color under its wings
and tail. However, that color differs depending on where this bird
lives, yellow for the east and red for the west.

Brown Pelican

(Pelecanus occidentalis)

The brown pelican was in danger of extinction in the 1960s due to the pesticide DDT. Once DDT was banned, this species made a tremendous resurgence.

Black-Capped Chickadee

(Poecile atricapillus)

Pay attention to the black-capped chickadee's distinctive call; the more "dee" is repeated at the end of "chickadee-dee-dee," the higher it thinks the threat is.

Cactus Wren

(Campylorhynchus brunneicapillus)

The cactus wren is well-adapted to the deserts of North America because it rarely drinks water, instead consuming enough liquids to survive by eating insects and fruit.

Mountain Bluebird

(Sialia currucoides)

The mountain bluebird nests in tree cavities excavated by woodpeckers. The scarcity of these cavities means that location is the most important quality for female mountain bluebirds when choosing a mate.

Western Meadowlark

(Sturnella neglecta)

Despite its name and coloring, the meadowlark is actually a member of the blackbird family. The only black part of a western meadowlark's pattern is the "V" shape on its chest.

Baltimore Oriole

(Icterus galbula)

Baltimore orioles are surprisingly picky when it comes to eating;
they only want dark-colored fruit, even when ripe, light-colored fruit
is available.

Great Horned Owl

(Bubo virginianus)

The great horned owl is a fierce predator that often hunts other birds, like the American crow, or even species larger than itself, such as ospreys, falcons, and other owls.

California Quail

(Callipepla californica)

The distinctive head plume on a California quail is actually six
feathers that overlap, making them look like one feather.

Scissor-Tailed Flycatcher

(Tyrannus forficatus)

The scissor-tailed flycatcher developed its long tail feathers to make quick turns in the air when chasing down its insectoid prey.

Northern Cardinal

(Cardinalis cardinalis)

You might be surprised to learn how aggressive northern cardinals can be. In spring, these birds might spend hours fighting other birds, or their own reflections, over territory.

Rhode Island Red

(Gallus gallus domesticus)

The Rhode Island red was bred in the late 19th century to be used both for meat and to lay eggs. Now, this chicken is mostly used to produce eggs.

Lark Bunting

(Calamospiza melanocorys)

When a bird sings while flying, it is called a "flight song." The lark bunting is unique in that it has two of such calls, one main song and one song for when males fight.

Ruffed Grouse

(Bonasa umbellus)

The male ruffed grouse has a display called "drumming on air" where it moves its wings back and forth rapidly, creating a sound akin to a car engine.

Northern Mockingbird

(Mimus polyglottos)

Because of its variety of songs, mockingbirds were coveted as pets in the 19th century. This high demand nearly wiped out all northern mockingbirds from the East Coast.

71

Blue Hen Chicken

(Gallus gallus domesticus)

Though this bird is not a recognized chicken breed, the folktale of an American Revolution captain carrying blue hens into battle gave it enough clout to become the state bird of Delaware.

Hermit Thrush. © Crista Forest, *www.foreststudios.com*. From *Birds at Home, Revised Edition* © Design Originals, *www.D-Originals.com*

73

Hermit Thrush

(Catharus guttatus)

The scientific name "guttatus" means spotted, referring to the markings on the hermit thrush's breast. This camouflage is useful when it forages on the ground for insects.

Ring-Necked Pheasant

(Phasianus colchicus)

The ring-necked pheasant has become a popular game bird over the years, but it was only introduced to North America from China in the 1880s.

77

Purple Finch

(Haemorhous purpureus)

Purple finches typically live in cool climates, but they have been
pushed farther north due to competition with house finches, which
have been winning in a battle for territory.

79

Eastern Bluebird

(Sialia sialis)

Eastern bluebirds began to decline in the early 20th century due
to loss of habitat; however, an effort to increase birdhouses has
effectively raised the bluebird population.

Atlantic Puffin

(Fratercula arctica)

Atlantic puffins are the provincial bird of Newfoundland and
Labrador because a large percentage of this bird population breeds
in Witless Bay, Newfoundland, Canada.

Northern
Mockingbird

(Mimus polyglottos)

The mockingbird loves to sing; it calls day and night from February
to November and learns new songs throughout its life, typically
mimicking other birds.

Northern Mockingbird. © Crista Forest, *www.foreststudios.com*. From *Birds at Home, Revised Edition* © Desi

American Goldfinch

(Spinus tristis)

Since these birds are used to hanging onto the stems of flexible
weeds, such as thistles and milkweed, American goldfinches are not
bothered when bird feeders and seed socks are jostled by the wind.

Western Meadowlark. © Crista Forest, *www.foreststudios.com*. From *Birds at Home, Revised Edition* © Design Originals, *www.D-Originals.com* 87

Western Meadowlark

(Sturnella neglecta)

During his famous expedition across the West, Meriwether Lewis discovered the western meadowlark, which is nearly identical to what is now known as the eastern meadowlark.